WOLFGANG AMADEUS MOZART

KONZERT

für Klavier und Orchester / for Piano and Orchestra

Nr. 20
d-Moll / D minor
KV 466

Ausgabe für 2 Klaviere
Edition for 2 Pianos

Kadenzen von / Cadenzas by
Ludwig van Beethoven · Christian Zacharias

Herausgegeben von / Edited by
Christoph Wolff · Christian Zacharias

Klavier II (Orchester) von / Piano II (Orchestra) by
Kurt Soldan

ALLE RECHTE VORBEHALTEN · ALL RIGHTS RESERVED

EDITION PETERS
LEIPZIG · LONDON · NEW YORK

Vorbemerkung

Das Klavierkonzert in d-Moll (KV 466) schrieb Mozart für die Subskriptionskonzerte der Fastenzeit des Jahres 1785. Laut Eintrag im eigenhändigen Werkverzeichnis des Komponisten wurde es am 10. Februar 1785 fertiggestellt und bereits am Tage darauf erstmals aufgeführt. Dazu bemerkte der seinerzeit in Wien weilende Leopold Mozart in einem Brief vom 14. Februar an seine Tochter: „*... ein neues vortreffliches Clavierconcert von Wolfgang, wo der Copist, da wir ankamen, noch daran abschrieb und dein Bruder das Rondo noch nicht einmal durchzuspielen Zeit hatte, weil er die Copiatur übersehen mußte.*" Wie die originale Notation der Takte 88 ff. des ersten Satzes belegt, benutzte Mozart für den Konzertvortrag ein Pedalklavier. Der Programmzettel für die Aufführung des C-Dur-Konzerts KV 467 vom 10. März 1785 erwähnt ausdrücklich, daß Mozart „*ein besonders grosses Forte piano Pedal beym Phantasieren gebrauchen wird ...*"

Die vorliegende Ausgabe wurde nach der autographen Partitur im Archiv der Gesellschaft für Musikfreunde, Wien *(Signatur: VII 3405)*, und unter Vergleich mit dem Erstdruck (J. André, Offenbach 1796; Verlags-Nr. 923) redigiert. Originale Kadenzen zu diesem Konzert, die sich in einem Brief Leopold Mozarts vom 8. April 1785 erwähnt finden („*Ich werde 2 neue Concerte [KV 466 und 467], dann alle Cadenzen mit bringen, habe alles schon in Händen.*"), sind nicht erhalten geblieben. Der Anhang dieser Ausgabe bietet darum u. a. die Kadenzen Beethovens (WoO 58), der Mozarts d-Moll-Konzert erstmals 1795 in Wien öffentlich vorgetragen hatte (L. van Beethoven, *Werke*, Serie IX/Band 2, Nr. 11–12). Die Partie des Soloklavieres von KV 466 entspricht in allen Einzelheiten dem Notentext der Originalquellen. Der Klavierauszug der Orchesterbegleitung (Klavier II) wurde in Dynamik und Artikulation der Originalpartitur weitestgehend angeglichen. Den Quellen nicht entstammende Zusätze sind durch Kleindruck (Bögen durch Strichelung) kenntlich gemacht.

Christoph Wolff

Prefatory Note

Mozart wrote his Piano Concerto in D minor, K. 466, for his subscription concerts held during the Lenten season of 1785. According to the entry in his own autograph catalogue of works, it was completed on 10 February 1785 and given its première one day later. Leopold Mozart, then visiting in Vienna, mentioned the piece in a letter of 14 February to his daughter: "*An excellent new piano concerto by Wolfgang was being written out by the copyist when we arrived, and your brother had not even had time to play through the Rondo as he had to supervise the work of copying.*" The original notation of bars 88 ff. in the first movement reveal that Mozart used a pedal piano for his concert performance. The playbill for the C-major Concerto K. 467, performed on 10 March 1785, expressly mentions that Mozart "*will use an especially large pedal fortepiano for his improvisations*".

The present edition has been revised on the basis of the autograph score located in the Gesellschaft der Musikfreunde in Vienna *(manuscript no. VII 3405)*. For comparison purposes we have also consulted the first edition issued in 1796 by J. André in Offenbach (publisher's no. 923). Original cadenzas for this concerto are mentioned in a letter written by Leopold Mozart on 8 April 1785: "*I will bring along all the cadenzas for the two new concertos [K. 455 and 467], which are already in my possession.*" These cadenzas have not survived. In the appendix of our edition we have therefore included, among other things, the cadenzas by Beethoven (WoO 58), who gave the first public performance of Mozart's D-minor Concerto in Vienna in 1795 (L. van Beethoven: *Werke*, series IX, volume 2, nos. 11–12). The solo piano part of K. 466 is identical in all respects to the text of the original sources. The piano reduction of the orchestral accompaniment (Piano II) has been made as consistent as possible with the original score as regards dynamics and articulation. Additions not contained in the sources are indicated by small type, or in the case of slurs by broken lines.

Christoph Wolff

INSTRUMENTE DES ORCHESTERS (Abkürzungen)
Bläser/winds (Bl.): Flauto (Fl.) – Oboe (Ob.) I/II – Fagotto (Fg.) I/II – Corno (Cor.) I/II – Tromba (Tr.) I/II – Timpani (Timp.)
Streicher/strings (Str.): Violino (Vl.) I/II – Viola (Va.) I/II – Violoncello (Vc.) – Basso (B.)

Aufführungsdauer / Duration: ca. 35 Min.

KONZERT
für Klavier und Orchester d-Moll Nr. 20
KV 466

W. A. Mozart (1756-1791)

Herausgegeben von
Christoph Wolff und Christian Zacharias

*) Siehe Vorbemerkung/see Prefatory Note

*) Kadenz von L. v. Beethoven siehe S. 81; Kadenzvorschlag des Herausgebers siehe S. 85.
Cadenza by L. v. Beethoven see p. 81; an additional cadenza by the editor is found on p. 85.

Auszierungsvorschlag bis T. 55/*suggested ornamentation until bar 55:*

*) Ausführungsvorschlag bei col Basso-Spiel:
   Suggested execution if the solo
   piano plays col basso:

56

31723

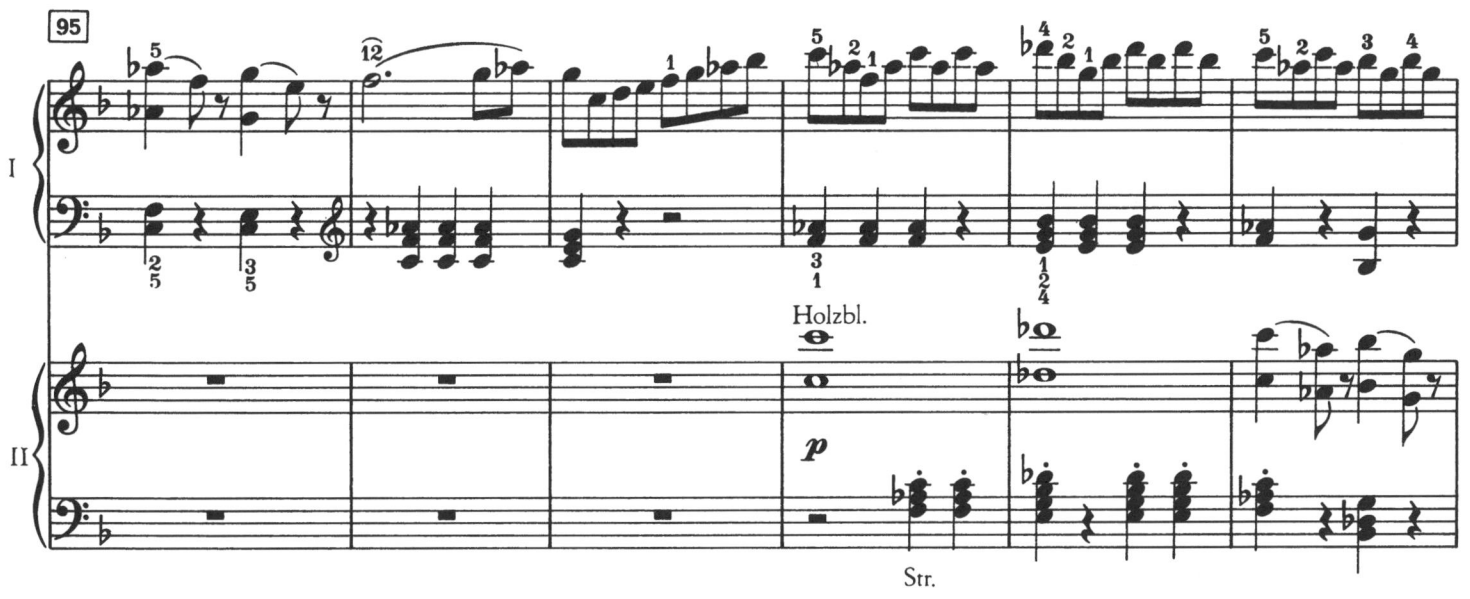
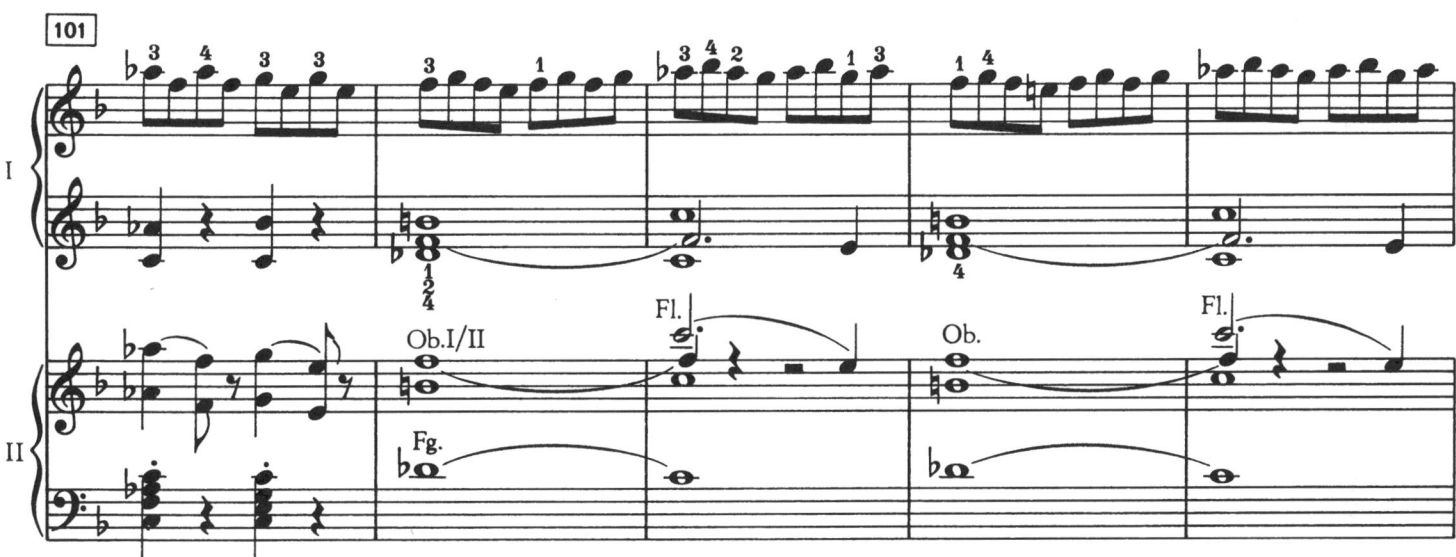
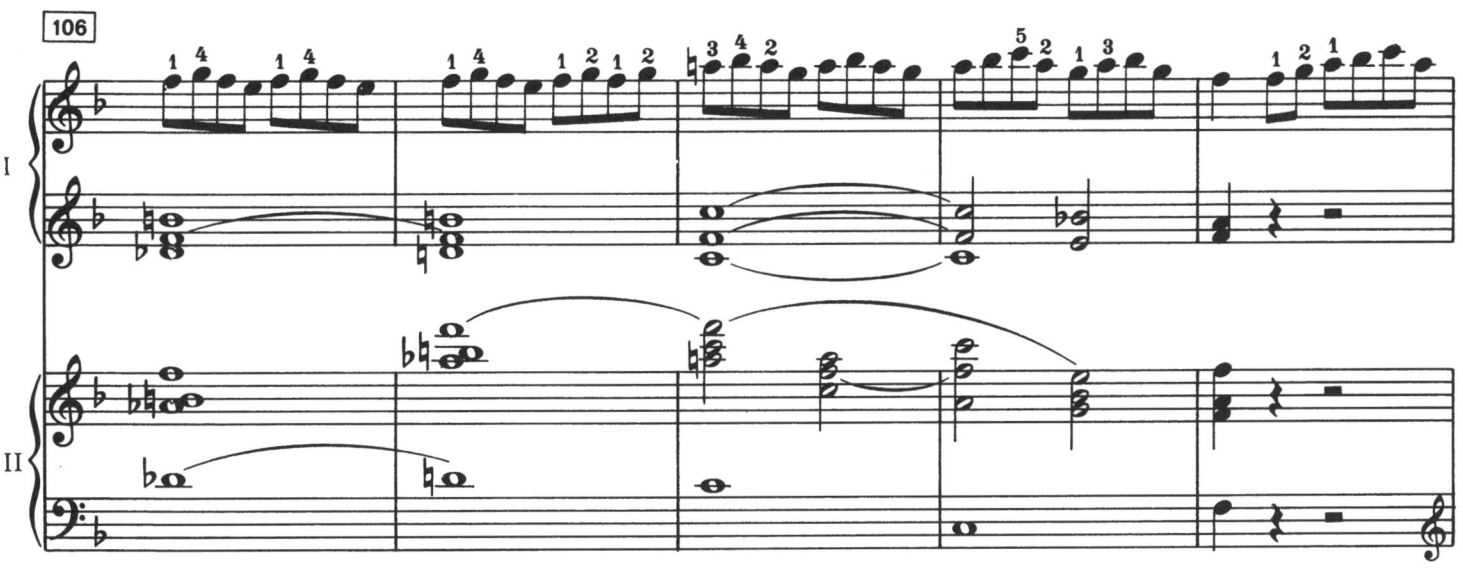

*) Ausführungsvorschlag/*suggested execution:*

*) Kadenz von L. v. Beethoven siehe S. 84; Kadenzvorschlag des Herausgebers siehe S. 87.
Cadenza by L. v. Beethoven see p. 84; an additional cadenza by the editor is found on p. 87.

ANHANG
Kadenz zum ersten Satz

L. van Beethoven
WoO 58

Kadenz zum dritten Satz

L. van Beethoven

Kadenz zum ersten Satz

Christian Zacharias

Kadenz zum dritten Satz

Christian Zacharias

Zur Interpretation

Der Umgang mit dem von allen späteren Zutaten gereinigten Urtext setzt mehr musikalisches Wissen und mehr Phantasie voraus als das Vertrauen auf eine Ausgabe mit Interpretationshilfen des Herausgebers. Jedoch soll auch eine Urtextausgabe den jeweiligen Interpretations- und Rezeptionsstand widerspiegeln. Aus diesem Grunde sei auf vier Aspekte der Annäherung an diesen Text eingegangen.

1. *Fingersätze:* Ziel war, so sparsam wie möglich zu bezeichnen, Fingersätze anzubieten, die vielleicht auf den ersten Blick ungewöhnlich anmuten, die aber dem plastischen Gestalten entgegenkommen, wobei eine kleinteilige Artikulation angestrebt wird, ohne daß dadurch übergeordnete große Bögen verloren gehen. Ausschließlich perlendes Spiel entspricht nicht mehr heutiger Aufführungspraxis, vielmehr wird das Sprechende, Deklamatorische des Dramatikers Mozart stärker zu Bewußtsein gebracht. Man sollte sich vergegenwärtigen, daß Mozart auch immer Bläser, Streicher und die menschliche Stimme im Sinn hat, wenn er seine musikalischen Ideen entwickelt. Kantables Spiel ist ebenso gefordert, wie deutliches Akzentuieren und Pointieren. Auch das Atemholen der Bläser und die Bogenführung der Streicher, z. B. ein Bogenwechsel, lassen sich durch Fingersätze ausdrücken. Daher findet der Benutzer z. B. zweimal denselben Finger bei benachbarten Tasten oder gar bewußt unbequeme Fingersätze, die ihn zwingen, ein Luftloch zu machen, neu anzusetzen.

2. *Verzierungen, Eingänge etc.:* Bei der Behandlung des Textes an sich, d. h., der Freiheit, Verzierungen anzubringen, Veränderungen vorzunehmen und – einen Schritt weiter – Eingänge und Überleitungen zu improvisieren oder festzulegen, werden gegebenermaßen vor allem persönliche Disposition und Laune, persönlicher Einfallsreichtum und Geschmack über das Resultat entscheiden. Angesichts der Tatsache, daß jedoch viele Spieler bei Fermatentakten Ratlosigkeit zeigen, sind an den wichtigsten Stellen erprobte und gespielte Veränderungen und Eingänge zur Diskussion gestellt. Vorbild war dabei Mozart selbst, der eine Auszierung nicht nur als Dekoration begreift, sondern als ein Mittel, die musikalische Gestalt treffender, reicher und schöner als das niedergeschriebene Original entstehen zu lassen. Ein typisches Beispiel hierfür ist der 2. Satz des Konzerts D-Dur, KV 451, T. 56 ff. und der dazugehörige Brief vom 9. Juni 1784. Der Herausgeber hat nicht versucht, einen zu zeitgebundenen Auszierungsstil anzubieten, wie gewisse, auf Mozart selbst zurückgehende Versionen langsamer Sonatensätze aufweisen (z. B. Klaviersonaten KV 332, 2. Satz und KV 284, 3. Satz, Adagio-Variation). Mozarts Werk zeigt, daß er diesem opulenten, vielleicht publikumswirksamen Stil immer mehr abgeschworen hat. Zeugnisse seines viel schlichteren, gleichwohl ergreifenderen Auszierens oder Veränderns finden sich außer in dem schon erwähnten langsamen Satz von KV 451, beispielsweise im 2. Satz der Klaviersonate c-moll KV 457 und im Rondo KV 494. Die Vorgehensweise hängt im übrigen sehr vom Stand der Niederschrift ab. Flüchtig notierte Werke, wie etwa KV 537 bedürfen grundsätzlich eines größeren Engagements seitens des Interpreten als sorgfältig niedergeschriebene.

3. *Kadenzen:* Die Gestalt der beigegebenen Kadenzen in dieser Editionsreihe (soweit keine Originalkadenzen vorliegen) ergab sich aus dem Versuch, dem Besonderen und Typischen an Mozarts eigenen Kadenzen nachzuspüren. Charakteristisch an der Mozartschen Kadenz ist die erstaunliche Ökonomie der Mischung aus prägnanten Spielformen, gelegentlichen weitergeführten Virtuositätsfloskeln und wenigen Überbleibseln eines musikalisch besonders ansprechenden Gedankens, oft des Seitenthemas. Seine Kadenz schiebt häufig eine sich aufdrängende Lösung auf oder verweigert sie sogar, um dafür einen unerwarteten Seitenpfad einzuschlagen. Bei weitgehendem Verzicht auf Modulationen und auf Reihung zusammenhangloser Neueinfälle hat Mozarts Kadenz, die nicht zu kurz und vor allem nie zu lang ausfällt, nicht selten die Funktion eines tönenden Geschenks und erfährt dadurch eigentlich erst ihre Rechtfertigung. Der große Zusammenhang ist jedoch nicht außer acht zu lassen, denn die Kadenz ist als eine geistreiche Eskapade in einem größeren Ganzen zu sehen, wo auch der Solist nur primus inter pares auftritt.

4. *Col-Basso-Spiel:* Noch Beethoven notiert in seinen Klavierkonzerten den Orchesterbaß in der linken Hand des Soloklaviers bei Tutti-Stellen, erst ab dem frühromantischen Virtuosenkonzert (J. N. Hummel) wird die Trennung Solo–Tutti endgültig vollzogen. Auf dem modernen Konzertflügel wird man jedoch in der Regel auf das Col-Basso-Spiel verzichten. Insbesondere wenn der Ausführende auf einem Hammerklavier spielt und ihm für die frühen Mozart-Konzerte ein kleineres Ensemble gegenübersteht, empfiehlt sich das Mitspielen der Tutti. Gemäß dem historischen Kontext sind dann die Solopassagen mit reduzierter Streicherbesetzung (jeweils nur 1 Pult) zu begleiten. Wie bei den meisten Fragen der Aufführungspraxis sollte auch hier behutsam nach den Gegebenheiten entschieden und am klingenden Resultat gemessen werden.

Zur vorliegenden Ausgabe:

Zum Kopfsatz des d-Moll-Konzerts KV 466 schrieb Beethoven eine Kadenz, die in der Folgezeit einen gewissen Modellcharakter für Kadenzen zu Mozart-Konzerten annahm. Es kann jedoch nicht übersehen werden, daß Mozarts Kadenztyp, der sich durch diskontinuierliche, assoziative Reihung auszeichnet, in starkem stilistischen Gegensatz steht zu Beethovens „kompositionellem" Vorgehen, das in logisch geradezu zwingender Weise alles folgerichtig auseinander hervorgehen läßt. Als Alternative folgt hier daher der Vorschlag einer Kadenz, die sich nicht am 19. Jahrhundert, sondern an den Mozartschen Fantasien orientiert und sogar Elemente des Stils C. Ph. E. Bachs einbezieht.

Die Forderung nach Beseitigung romantischen Ballasts umfaßt auch die Bewußtmachung des ¢-Takts der Romance. Ein fließendes Andante-Tempo, das auch dem g-Moll-Mittelteil gerecht wird, dürfte bei ♩ = 46–48 anzusetzen sein.

Christian Zacharias

Notes on Performance

More imagination and a greater knowledge of music are required of a performer when he uses an *Urtext* edition expunged of all later accretions than when he simply trusts an edition with performance instructions supplied by the editor. None the less, even an *Urtext* edition should mirror the current state of knowledge of musical performance and reception. For this reason, four points should be borne in mind when approaching this text.

1. *Fingering:* The goal was to keep fingering to a minimum, but to indicate fingerings which may perhaps seem unconventional at first glance but which help to capture the plastic form of the music. An attempt has been made to render details of articulation without sacrificing large-scale phrasing. Performing practice today no longer demands *jeu perlé* but rather a stronger emphasis on the rhetorical and declamatory aspects of Mozart's music, the art of a born dramatist. It should be remembered that Mozart always had winds, strings and the human voice in mind when he developed his musical ideas. Cantabile playing is no less a requirement than clear accentuation and articulation. Even the breathing pauses required of wind instruments or the bowing of strings (e. g. changes of bow) can be expressed in the fingering. Thus, the user may find the same finger used successively on adjoining keys, or even a deliberately clumsy fingering that forces him to take a breath and begin a new attack.

2. *Ornamentation, entrances, etc.:* It is largely the personal disposition and mood of the player, his ingenuity and taste, that will guide him in dealing with the text itself, that is, the freedom with which he renders ornaments, introduces variations and, one step further, improvises or writes out entrances and transitions. Considering, however, that many players fall into a quandary when confronted by a fermata measure, a number of tried and tested options for variations and entrances have been presented for the most important passages. Here the editor has taken as his guide Mozart himself, who viewed embellishments not merely as decoration but also as a means to make his music richer, more striking and more beautiful than in the written-out original. One typical example of this is provided by measures 56 ff. in the second movement of the D-major Concerto K 451, together with Mozart's letter of 9 June 1784. The editor has not attempted to offer a style of ornamentation which is too closely bound to Mozart's own age, as revealed, for example, in certain versions of slow movements traceable to Mozart himself (see, for example, in his piano sonatas the second movement of K 332 or the third movement, Adagio and Variation, of K 284). Mozart's oeuvre shows that he increasingly tended to reject this opulent, perhaps slightly grandstanding style of ornamentation. Evidence of a more straightforward and, at the same time, more moving style of ornamentation and variation is provided not only by the aforementioned slow movement of K 451 but also by the second movement of the C-minor Sonata K 457 and the Rondo K 494. Our approach, moreover, is governed by the state of the manuscript copy. Hastily notated works, such as K 537, generally demand greater commitment on the part of the performer than do works in carefully notated fair copies.

3. *Cadenzas:* The cadenzas supplied in this series (wherever no original cadenzas exist) result from an attempt to recapture the idiosyncratic and characteristic aspects of Mozart's own cadenzas. Typically, Mozart's cadenzas reveal an astonishing economy, mingling terse performance formulas, occasionally extended virtuoso flourishes and a few remnants of a particularly winning musical idea, often taken from the second theme. His cadenzas often postpone, or even withhold, an impending resolution of the harmony in order to strike out on an unwonted byway. By generally avoiding modulations and strings of unrelated new ideas, Mozart's cadenzas, which seem neither too short and never too long, quite frequently assume the function and *raison d'être* of a musical gift to the listener. However, the performer should never ignore the larger context, for the cadenza should be viewed as an ingenious escapade within a larger whole in which the soloist only appears as the *primus inter pares*, the first among equals.

4. *Playing »col basso«:* Even Beethoven, in the tutti sections of his piano concertos, wrote out the orchestral bass line in the left hand of the piano part; not until the early romantic virtuoso concertos of J. N. Hummel was the separation of solo and tutti complete. On a modern concert grand, we generally prefer not to play *col basso*; when, however, the pianist is using a *Hammerklavier*, particularly in the earlier Mozart concertos, and is accompanied by a small ensemble, it is advisable to play along with the tutti. In this case, as dictated by the historical context, the solo passages should be accompanied by a reduced string section (one desk each). As in most questions of performing practice, here, too, the player should make his decisions judiciously, given the circumstances involved, and judge them by the acoustical results.

Remarks on the present edition:

For the opening movement of the D-minor Concerto, K. 466, Beethoven wrote a cadenza which later virtually assumed examplary status for cadenzas in Mozart concertos. There is, however, no overlooking the fact that Mozart's brand of cadenza, being a discontinnous and associative series of musical ideas, is stylistically the opposite of Beethoven's "compositional" approach, in which the musical events emerge organically with an almost relentless logic. As an alternative suggestion we have therefore included a cadenza orientated not on the nineteenth century but rather on Mozart's own fantasies and even containing elements of the style of C. P. E. Bach.

Players who wish to disembarrass Mozart's music of its romantic ballast should also pay attention to the ¢ metre of the Romance. This should probably be taken at ♩ = 46–48, a tempo which is also appropriate to the middle section in G minor.

Christian Zacharias